System Administrator Guide

Practical Guide

A. De Quattro

System Administrator Guide

Chapter 1: What is a System Administrator?

A System Administrator, often abbreviated as SysAdmin, is a professional responsible for managing, maintaining, and overseeing a company's systems, particularly its computers and networks. The role is critical for ensuring that systems operate smoothly and securely, contributing to an organization's productivity and efficiency. This chapter will cover the fundamental roles and responsibilities of a System Administrator, as well as provide practical examples that will illustrate these concepts step by step.

Role and Responsibilities

The primary duties of a System Administrator include:

1. **System Installation and Configuration**: Setting up hardware and software systems,

which includes operating systems, applications, and network configurations.

Example: If a company decides to implement a new Windows Server, a SysAdmin would be responsible for installing the server operating system from scratch, configure domain settings, and set up basic security policies.

Step-by-Step:

- Obtain the Windows Server installation media (USB/DVD).

- Boot the server from the installation media and follow the prompts.

- Select the appropriate installation options, including language and edition.

- Configure the server roles needed (e.g., Domain Controller, File Server).

- Set up user permissions and access controls following company policy.

2. **System Monitoring**: Keeping an eye on servers and networks to ensure they operate efficiently. This often includes checking system performance metrics, logs, and alerts.

   Example: Monitoring CPU usage, memory load, and network traffic to identify potential issues before they escalate.

   Step-by-Step:

   - Utilize monitoring tools like Nagios, Zabbix, or SolarWinds.

   - Set up alerts for unusual activity (e.g., CPU usage exceeding 90%).

   - Regularly check logs for system errors or warnings using tools like Splunk or ELK Stack.

   - Analyze performance data to identify trends that could indicate emerging problems.

3. **User Management**: Creating and

managing user accounts, including setting permissions and access controls.

   Example: When new employees join the company, it is the SysAdmin's job to create their accounts on various systems (email, databases, etc.).

   Step-by-Step:

   - Access the Active Directory Users and Computers (ADUC) console.

   - Select the appropriate organizational unit (OU) for the new user.

   - Right-click and select "New" -> "User".

   - Provide necessary details such as first name, last name, and username.

   - Assign appropriate permissions based on user roles.

4. **Backup and Recovery**: Implementing data backup solutions to prevent data loss and

establishing recovery procedures in case of a disaster.

Example: Setting up automated backups for critical databases and creating a recovery plan to restore data in case of system failure.

Step-by-Step:

- Choose a backup solution (e.g., Acronis, Veeam).

- Schedule regular backups (daily/weekly) for databases and file systems.

- Store backups securely in an off-site location or cloud platform.

- Test the recovery process regularly to ensure data can be restored without issues.

5. **Security Management**: Implementing security measures to protect the systems from unauthorized access and malware.

Example: Configuring firewalls, setting up antivirus software, and monitoring for security breaches.

Step-by-Step:

- Install a firewall (e.g., pfSense, Cisco ASA) and configure rules based on company needs.

- Deploy antivirus solutions (e.g., Norton, McAfee) across all endpoints.

- Regularly update all security software and operating systems to patch vulnerabilities.

- Conduct security audits to identify weaknesses in the current setup.

6. **Software Updates and Patch Management**: Ensuring that all software and operating systems are up-to-date with the latest patches.

Example: Automating updates for operating systems and applications to minimize security risks.

Step-by-Step:

- Utilize tools like WSUS (Windows Server Update Services) or SCCM (System Center Configuration Manager) to manage updates.

- Schedule regular maintenance windows for applying updates.

- Monitor compliance to ensure that all systems are updated on time.

- Document changes and maintain a log of updates applied.

7. **Network Configuration and Management**: Setting up and maintaining the organization's network environment, including routers, switches, and load balancers.

Example: Configuring a new VLAN to

segment network traffic for improved performance and security.

Step-by-Step:

- Access network switch configuration (via console or SSH).

- Create a new VLAN by specifying a VLAN ID and name.

- Assign switch ports to the new VLAN based on departmental needs.

- Update routing protocols if necessary to ensure proper traffic flow.

8. **Documentation**: Maintaining thorough documentation of system configurations, procedures, and policies.

Example: Creating a wiki or knowledge base that contains troubleshooting guides, network diagrams, and standard operating procedures (SOPs).

Step-by-Step:

- Use tools like Confluence, SharePoint, or Google Docs to document detailed procedures.

- Create a structured template for consistent documentation (e.g., issue type, steps to resolve, affected systems).

- Regularly review and update documentation to ensure accuracy.

- Train team members on how to use documentation effectively.

Tools and Technologies

System Administrators utilize a variety of tools and technologies to manage and maintain systems effectively. Here are some commonly used tools:

- **Operating Systems**: Windows Server,

Linux distributions (e.g., Ubuntu, CentOS), and Mac OS.

- **Monitoring Tools**: Nagios, Zabbix, SolarWinds, Datadog.

- **Backup Solutions**: Acronis, Veeam, Commvault.

- **Network Management**: Cisco IOS, pfSense, Wireshark.

- **Configuration Management**: Ansible, Puppet, Chef.

- **Virtualization Technologies**: VMware, Hyper-V, Docker.

- **Scripting Languages**: PowerShell, Bash, Python.

Understanding System Administrator Roles in Different Environments

The role of a System Administrator can vary based on the organization's size, industry type, and specific needs. Here are a few scenarios:

1. **Small Business Environment**: In a small company, a SysAdmin may handle a wide range of responsibilities including hardware installations, user support, and network management all by themselves.

2. **Large Enterprise Environment**: In larger companies, there may be specialized SysAdmins focusing on specific areas such as database administration, network security, or cloud infrastructures.

3. **Managed Service Providers (MSP)**: SysAdmins may work for an MSP which provides IT services for multiple clients, requiring them to manage and support diverse systems and environments.

4. **Cloud Services**: With the advent of cloud computing, SysAdmins are increasingly required to manage cloud-based resources, requiring knowledge of platforms like AWS, Azure, or Google Cloud.

The System Administrator plays a pivotal role in today's technology-driven workplaces by ensuring that all systems are up and running efficiently, securely, and effectively. This chapter has outlined the fundamental concepts of what a SysAdmin does, their responsibilities, the tools they use, and the diverse environments in which they may work. In the following chapters, we will delve deeper into each of these areas with detailed examples, best practices, and real-world scenarios to illustrate the complexities and nuances of the SysAdmin profession.

Chapter 2: Prerequisites and Fundamental Skills

As a System Administrator, a wide array of knowledge and skills is essential to manage and maintain systems effectively. In this chapter, we will delve into the key prerequisites and fundamental skills required to excel in this role. Each section will cover necessary concepts, practical examples, and step-by-step instructions to help you build a solid foundation in system administration.

2.1. Basic Computer Knowledge

Basic computer knowledge forms the cornerstone of a System Administrator's skill set. It includes an understanding of operating systems, hardware components, software applications, and troubleshooting techniques. Here, we will break down each area and demonstrate practical applications for each.

Understanding Operating Systems

A System Administrator must understand how different operating systems function, including Windows, Linux, and macOS.

Example: Installing Ubuntu Linux

1. **Download the ISO:**

   - Go to the [Ubuntu website] (https://ubuntu.com/download).

   - Select the version (LTS is recommended for stability).

   - Click "Download."

2. **Create Bootable USB:**

   - Use a tool like Rufus (for Windows) or Etcher (multi-platform).

   - Insert a USB drive and launch Rufus.

   - Select the downloaded ISO file and create

the bootable USB.

3. **Install Ubuntu:**

 - Boot your computer from the USB drive.

 - Select "Try Ubuntu" or "Install Ubuntu."

 - Follow the installation prompts (language, keyboard layout, etc.).

 - Select installation type (Erase disk for a clean install or dual-boot).

 - Set username and password, and proceed with the installation.

4. **Understand Commands:**

 - Familiarize yourself with basic Linux commands, like:

   - `ls` - List files.

   - `cd` - Change directory.

   - `cp` - Copy files.

   - `mv` - Move files.

- `rm` - Delete files.

Familiarity with Hardware Components

Understanding computer hardware is essential for diagnosing issues and performing upgrades.

Example: Identifying Components in a Desktop Computer

1. **Open the Case:**

   - Turn off the PC and unplug it.

   - Unscrew and remove the side panel.

2. **Identify Key Components:**

   - **CPU (Central Processing Unit):** Located under the heatsink/fan.

   - **RAM (Random Access Memory):** Long sticks inserted into slots on the motherboard.

- **Motherboard:** The main circuit board containing CPU and RAM slots, as well as expansion slots for additional components.

- **Power Supply Unit (PSU):** Converts mains AC to low-voltage regulated DC power for the internal components.

3. **Perform Basic Troubleshooting:**

- If the PC fails to boot, reseat RAM and check power connections.

- Monitor temperatures using BIOS/UEFI settings.

Software Applications

A System Administrator should be comfortable with various software tools for managing systems.

**Example: Using Remote Desktop Protocol

(RDP)**

1. **Enable RDP on a Windows Machine:**

   - Right-click on "This PC" and select "Properties."

   - Click on "Remote settings."

   - Check "Allow remote connections to this computer."

2. **Connect from Another Computer:**

   - Open Remote Desktop Connection (search for "mstsc").

   - Enter the IP address of the target computer.

   - Click "Connect" and enter the username/password when prompted.

3. **Troubleshooting RDP Connectivity:**

   - Ensure the firewall permits RDP connections.

   - Verify network connection between the

two devices.

2.2. Networking Skills and Protocols

Networking is a fundamental skill for any System Administrator. A strong understanding of networking principles and protocols allows administrators to configure, troubleshoot, and maintain networked systems.

Key Networking Concepts

1. **Understanding the Basics:**

   - **IP Addressing:** Know how IP addresses are assigned (static vs. dynamic).

   - **Subnetting:** Understand how IP addresses are divided into subnets.

Example: Calculate Subnets

- For a /24 subnet (e.g., 192.168.1.0/24):

    - Subnet mask: 255.255.255.0

    - Total addresses: 256 (0-255).

    - Usable addresses: 254 (1-254).

2. **Networking Hardware:**

   - **Routers:** Direct traffic between networks based on IP addresses.

   - **Switches:** Connect multiple devices on the same network.

   - **Firewalls:** Control incoming and outgoing traffic based on predetermined security rules.

3. **Common Networking Protocols:**

   - **TCP/IP:** The foundational protocol for networking, governing how data is sent over the internet.

   - **HTTP/HTTPS:** Protocols used for

web traffic. HTTPS adds encryption for security.

   - **FTP/SFTP:** Protocols for transferring files; SFTP adds a layer of security.

4. **Practical Example: Setting Up a Local Network**

   Step-by-Step: Basic Home Network Setup

   1. **Device Setup:**

      - Connect the modem to the router.

      - Connect wired devices (PCs) to the router using Ethernet cables.

   2. **Configuring the Router:**

      - Access the router by entering its IP address in a web browser (e.g., 192.168.1.1).

      - Input the admin credentials (default is

often "admin"/"admin").

  - Configure Wi-Fi settings, including SSID (network name) and password.

  3. **IP Configuration:**

  - Check the router interface for DHCP settings. Ensure this is enabled to dynamically assign IPs.

  - For a static IP setup, individually assign IP addresses to devices under router settings.

  4. **Testing Network Connectivity:**

  - Use the command `ping google.com` in the command line to check for internet connectivity.

  - Use `ipconfig` (Windows) or `ifconfig` (Linux) to check assigned IP addresses.

Advanced Networking Topics

- **Understanding VPNs:**

  - Virtual Private Networks provide secure access to a network over the internet, encrypting data between user devices and servers.

  - **Example: Setting Up a VPN Connection**

    1. Install VPN client software on your device.

    2. Configure the VPN settings by entering the server address, your credentials, and other necessary configurations.

    3. Connect to the VPN and verify your IP address has changed (e.g., using `whatismyip.com`).

2.3. Fundamentals of Cybersecurity

Cybersecurity is more crucial than ever as

threats become increasingly sophisticated. A System Administrator must have a foundational understanding of security principles, practices, and tools to safeguard systems and data.

Understanding Security Principles

1. **Confidentiality, Integrity, and Availability (CIA Triad):**

   - **Confidentiality:** Ensuring that information is not accessed by unauthorized users.

   - **Integrity:** Protecting information from being altered by unauthorized users.

   - **Availability:** Ensuring that information is accessible when needed.

2. **Common Cyber Threats:**

   - **Malware:** Malicious software designed to harm systems (viruses, worms, trojans).

- **Phishing:** Deceptive attempts to obtain sensitive information by masquerading as a trustworthy entity.

- **Denial-of-Service (DoS):** Attacks aimed at disrupting service availability.

Basic Security Practices

1. **Implementing Firewalls:**

   - Firewalls can be hardware-based (router/firewall appliances) or software-based (built-in firewall in operating systems).

   - **Example: Configuring Windows Firewall**

      - Go to Control Panel > System and Security > Windows Defender Firewall.

      - Choose "Advanced settings" to create inbound/outbound rules based on application, port, or protocol.

2. **Antivirus Solutions:**

- Install and maintain up-to-date antivirus software on all systems.

- Schedule regular scans to detect and remove malware.

3. **Data Encryption:**

- Encrypt sensitive data to prevent unauthorized access.

- **Example: Use BitLocker on Windows**

1. Right-click on the drive you want to encrypt.

2. Select "Turn on BitLocker" and follow the setup process.

4. **Regular Software Updates:**

- Keep all operating systems and software up to date to mitigate vulnerabilities.

- **Example: Automatic Updates on Windows**

- Go to Settings > Update & Security > Windows Update.

- Turn on "Get updates automatically."

Incident Response Planning

Being prepared for a security incident is vital.

1. **Creating an Incident Response Plan:**

   - Define roles and responsibilities.

   - Outline response procedures for different types of incidents (e.g., data breach, malware infection).

   - Include communication protocols and escalation procedures.

2. **Conducting Regular Security Drills:**

   - Simulate an incident to test the effectiveness of the response plan.

   - Analyze the results and adjust the plan for better preparedness.

2.4. Useful Programming Languages

While a System Administrator does not need to be a software developer, knowledge of certain programming languages can significantly enhance efficiency and automation.

Scripting Languages

1. **Bash Scripting:** Essential for automating tasks in Linux environments.

   - **Example: Creating a Simple Backup Script**

   ```bash
   #!/bin/bash
   # Backup script
   src="/path/to/source"
   ```

    dest="/path/to/destination"

    rsync -av --delete "$src" "$dest"

    ```

  - Save this as `backup.sh`, and run it via the
terminal with `bash backup.sh`.


2. **PowerShell:** A powerful scripting
language for Windows administration.

  - **Example: Listing Services**

    ```powershell

    Get-Service | Where-Object {$_.Status -eq
"Running"}

    ```

  - This command lists all running services in
Windows.

General-Purpose Programming
Languages

1. **Python:** Widely used for automation,
    ```

data manipulation, and more.

- **Example: A Simple HTTP Request**

```python
import requests


response = requests.get('http://example.com')

print(response.status_code)
```

- This script demonstrates how to make an HTTP GET request.

2. **JavaScript:** Understanding JavaScript can be useful for web-related tasks and Node.js environments.

- **Example: Simple Web Server Using Node.js**

```javascript
const http = require('http');
```

```
const server = http.createServer((req, res)
=> {

    res.statusCode = 200;

    res.setHeader('Content-Type', 'text/plain');

    res.end('Hello World\n');

});


server.listen(3000, () => {

    console.log('Server running at
http://localhost:3000/');

});
```

3. **SQL:** Important for database management.

   - **Example: Querying a Database**

   ```sql
   SELECT * FROM Users WHERE active =
1;
```

```
```

- This simple SQL statement retrieves active users from a database.

The prerequisites and fundamental skills outlined in this chapter provide a robust groundwork for aspiring System Administrators. Mastering basic computer knowledge, networking principles, cybersecurity fundamentals, and programming languages will prepare you for the multifaceted challenges of the role. Continue building on these skills, and you will have a strong foundation for a successful career in system administration.

Chapter 3: Training and Certifications

In the ever-evolving field of technology, particularly in areas related to system administration, it is paramount to possess a robust foundation of knowledge coupled with formal qualifications. This chapter delves into the significant aspects of training and certifications that can pave the way for a successful career as a system administrator (SysAdmin). It is structured into three distinct sections: recommended academic paths, professional certifications, and the importance of ongoing education through community engagement.

3.1 Recommended Academic Paths

When pursuing a career as a system administrator, a solid educational background is essential. While some can succeed without formal education, a degree often provides essential knowledge and skills. Here are some recommended academic paths:

3.1.1 Bachelor's Degree in Computer Science

A Bachelor's degree in Computer Science is one of the most common paths for aspiring system administrators. This program typically includes a comprehensive curriculum consisting of programming, algorithms, data structures, and systems architecture.

Step-by-step Example:

1. **Enrollment**: Begin by researching accredited universities offering Computer Science programs. Consider factors such as location, tuition cost, faculty experience, and campus resources. Once you find a suitable institution, go through the application process.

2. **Coursework**: During your studies, focus on courses like Operating Systems, Network Design, Database Management, and

Cybersecurity. Engage in practical lab sessions to gain hands-on experience.

3. **Projects**: Participate in group projects and internships. For example, you might work on setting up a network for a small business as part of a course project, giving you real-world experience.

4. **Graduation**: Successfully complete all required coursework and graduate with your degree.

3.1.2 Associate's Degree in Information Technology

An Associate's degree can serve as a quicker alternative. This two-year degree concentrates on practical skills and fundamental IT knowledge.

Step-by-Step Example:

1. **Enrollment**: Identify community colleges or technical schools that offer Associate's degrees in Information Technology. Make sure they have programs tailored specifically for systems administration.

2. **Core Subjects**: Study core subjects such as Introduction to Networking, Systems Administration Basics, and Security Fundamentals. This is where you'll learn about servers, Active Directory, and basic troubleshooting techniques.

3. **Hands-On Labs**: Take advantage of hands-on labs. For instance, you might work in a lab environment to set up Linux servers or troubleshoot Windows environments.

4. **Certification Preparation**: Use this time to prepare for foundational certifications like CompTIA A+ or Network+. Many community colleges offer non-credit workshops or

bootcamps that can help you prepare.

5. **Graduation**: Complete your degree, which can position you for entry-level positions in IT.

3.1.3 Specialized Programs and Bootcamps

For individuals seeking a faster route into system administration, specialized programs or bootcamps can be effective. These intensive courses focus on teaching specific skills in a short time, often catering directly to the job market.

Step-by-Step Example:

1. **Research Bootcamps**: Look for accredited online or in-person bootcamps that offer systems administration programs. Websites like CourseReport or CareerFoundry

can provide reviews.

2. **Curriculum**: Enroll in a bootcamp that covers vital areas including Linux Administration, Cloud Computing, and Scripting in languages like Python or Bash.

3. **Projects and Labs**: Throughout the bootcamp, work on projects that simulate real-world challenges, such as configuring a web server or deploying an application in a cloud environment.

4. **Networking**: Attend networking events and connect with professionals in the industry. Many bootcamps host meetups where you can meet potential employers.

5. **Job Placement Assistance**: Many bootcamps offer job placement services—leverage these resources to find opportunities after graduating.

3.2 Professional Certifications

Certifications are essential in validating your skills and knowledge as a system administrator. They demonstrate to potential employers that you have the necessary expertise to manage their IT infrastructure effectively. Here are some of the most recognized certifications in the field:

3.2.1 CompTIA A+

Description: CompTIA A+ is an entry-level certification that covers the fundamentals of IT support and troubleshooting.

Step-by-Step Example to Obtain CompTIA A+:

1. **Study Materials**: Acquire study materials, which can include books, online

courses, and practice exams. Websites like Pluralsight or Udemy are excellent for online learning.

2. **Enroll in an Online Course**: Consider completing a structured online course that guides you through the syllabus, covering topics like hardware, operating systems, and network troubleshooting.

3. **Practice Exams**: Before attempting the certification exams, take practice tests available through CompTIA's website or other platforms.

4. **Schedule the Exam**: Once you feel confident, schedule your exams through Pearson VUE or another authorized testing center.

5. **Exam Day**: Arrive with the necessary identification and materials. Complete both parts of the exam to earn your certification.

3.2.2 Microsoft Certified: Azure Administrator Associate

Description: This certification validates your skills in managing Azure subscriptions, implementing storage solutions, and configuring virtual networks.

Step-by-Step Example to Obtain Microsoft Certification:

1. **Prerequisites**: Familiarize yourself with the Azure platform through Microsoft Learn and other resources.

2. **Courses**: Enroll in a recommended course for Azure Administrator certification available on platforms like LinkedIn Learning or Coursera.

3. **Hands-on Experience**: Create a free Azure account and start practicing. Completing hands-on labs will help solidify your understanding of the Azure environment.

4. **Study Group**: Join a study group or community forum to exchange knowledge and tips about the certification exam.

5. **Schedule Exam**: Register for the exam via the Microsoft certification portal.

6. **Take the Exam**: On exam day, log into the testing platform and successfully complete the certification exam.

3.2.3 Cisco Certified Network Associate (CCNA)

Description: As networking skills are vital for SysAdmins, obtaining a CCNA certification from Cisco is beneficial. This credential covers a wide range of networking fundamentals.

Step-by-Step Example to Obtain CCNA:

1. **Prepare Study Material**: Gather study guides, books like "CCNA Routing and Switching" by Wendell Odom, and online resources.

2. **Networking Practice**: Use Cisco's Packet Tracer simulation tool to practice configuring networks and troubleshooting common issues.

3. **Online Courses**: Consider enrolling in an online course specific to CCNA preparation.

4. **Join Study Groups**: Participate in forums or local study groups focused on CCNA.

5. **Register for the Exam**: Schedule the
CCNA exam through Pearson VUE.

6. **Exam Day**: Complete the exam and
upon passing, you'll receive your CCNA
certification.

3.3 Ongoing Education and the Importance
of Communities

Given the rapid pace of technological
advancement, continuous education is vital for
success as a system administrator.

3.3.1 Staying Current with Technology

Technology is always changing, and new tools
and methodologies frequently emerge.
Ongoing education can take many forms:

1. **Online Courses**: Engage in platforms like Coursera, Udemy, and Pluralsight for up-to-date courses.

2. **Webinars and Conferences**: Attend webinars and industry conferences. Events like Microsoft Ignite and Cisco Live provide insights into the latest technology trends.

3. **Self-Directed Learning**: Establish a regular schedule to read blogs, white papers, and online articles about new technologies and industry trends.

3.3.2 The Value of Networking and Community Engagement

Building a professional network and engaging with communities can significantly enhance your career prospects.

1. **Join Professional Associations**:

Consider joining associations such as the System Administrators Guild (SAGE) or the Association for Computing Machinery (ACM). Membership often provides access to resources and networking opportunities.

2. **Participate in Online Forums**: Engage in platforms like Spiceworks or Reddit's SysAdmin subreddit. These communities allow you to ask questions, share knowledge, and connect with other industry professionals.

3. **Contribute to Open Source Projects**: Participating in open-source projects is a fantastic way to learn new skills, collaborate with others, and showcase your abilities to potential employers.

4. **Attend Local Meetups**: Explore local tech meetups or user groups in your area. These informal gatherings can help you learn from peers and expand your network.

5. **Mentorship**: Seek mentors who can provide guidance, advice, and insights based on their experiences. You can also consider becoming a mentor yourself.

Embarking on a career as a system administrator requires a strong educational foundation, relevant certifications, and commitment to lifelong learning. By pursuing recommended academic paths, obtaining professional certifications, and engaging with the tech community, you can position yourself for success in this dynamic field. The combination of formal education, practical experience, and ongoing professional development can propel you toward a fulfilling career as a system administrator.

Chapter 4: Tools and Technologies

In the realm of System Administration, having a robust understanding of the tools and technologies of the trade is essential. In this chapter, we'll explore various systems, virtualization methods, monitoring tools, and backup strategies that are critical to effective system administration. Whether you're managing servers or client machines, these tools will help you maintain a secure, efficient, and responsive IT environment.

4.1. Operating Systems: Windows, Linux, macOS

Operating systems form the backbone of any computing environment. As a System Administrator, you are likely to encounter a variety of operating systems including Windows, Linux, and macOS. Each OS has its own strengths, weaknesses, and use cases.

Windows

Windows is widely used in enterprise environments and offers a straightforward user interface. Here are some practical steps you might take when managing a Windows environment:

Example 1: User Account Management in Windows

1. **Open Active Directory Users and Computers (ADUC):**

   - Go to `Start` > `Administrative Tools` > `Active Directory Users and Computers`.

2. **Create a New User:**

   - In the console, right-click the organizational unit (OU) where you want to create the user, and click `New` > `User`.

   - Fill in the First name, Last name, and

Logon name, then click `Next`.

3. **Set Password:**

   - Enter the password for the user and configure options for requiring a password change on next login if desired. Click `Next`, then `Finish`.

4. **Assign Permissions:**

   - Right-click the user's account, and select `Properties`.

   - Go to the `Member Of` tab to add the user to security groups based on their role.

Linux

Linux is an open-source operating system popular in server environments for its stability and flexibility.

Example 2: Adding a New User in Linux

1. **Open Terminal:**

   - Access the terminal interface of your Linux machine.

2. **Create a New User:**

   - Use the command `sudo adduser username`, replacing `username` with the desired account name.

3. **Set Password:**

   - Follow the prompts to create a password for the new user.

4. **Configure User Permissions:**

   - If the user needs sudo privileges, run `sudo usermod -aG sudo username`.

5. **Verify User Creation:**

- Use the command `getent passwd username` to confirm user details.

macOS

macOS combines a user-friendly interface with Unix underpinnings, making it favored for development environments and among creative professionals.

Example 3: Managing Users on macOS

1. **Open System Preferences:**

   - Click on the Apple logo in the top left and select `System Preferences`.

2. **Go to Users & Groups:**

   - Click `Users & Groups` to view existing users.

3. **Add a New User:**

   - Click the lock icon to make changes, then click the `+` button below the user list.

   - Choose the account type (Admin, Standard, Managed), fill in the user details, and click `Create User`.

4. **Reset Password:**

   - If a user forgets their password, use the `Reset Password` option under the same `Users & Groups` pane.

4.2. Virtualization and Containerization

Virtualization and containerization are pivotal for resource optimization and application isolation in modern IT environments.

Virtualization

Virtualization allows you to create virtual instances of servers or desktops. Tools like VMware, Hyper-V, and VirtualBox are popular choices.

Example 4: Creating a Virtual Machine with VirtualBox

1. **Download and Install VirtualBox:**

   - Get the installer from the VirtualBox official website and complete the installation.

2. **Launch VirtualBox:**

   - Click on `New` to create a new VM.

3. **Configure VM Settings:**

   - Choose the name, type (Linux/Windows), and version of OS.

   - Allocate RAM and create a new virtual hard disk.

4. **Install the Operating System:**

   - Boot the VM and select the ISO for the OS installation.

   - Follow the OS installation prompts to complete the setup.

Containerization

Containerization, primarily achieved through Docker, allows you to deploy applications in isolated environments known as containers.

Example 5: Getting Started with Docker

1. **Install Docker:**

   - Follow platform-specific instructions to install Docker on your machine.

2. **Pull a Docker Image:**

- Use the command `docker pull ubuntu:latest` to get the latest Ubuntu image.

3. **Run a Docker Container:**

   - Execute `docker run -it ubuntu:latest` to create and access a new container instance.

4. **Install Applications:**

   - Inside the container, you can install any required packages. For example, `apt-get update` followed by `apt-get install -y nginx`.

5. **Persistent Data:**

   - Use Docker volumes to persist data. For example, `docker run -v /host/path:/container/path -it ubuntu:latest`.

4.3. Monitoring and Management Tools

Ensuring that systems operate smoothly

requires constant monitoring and effective management tools. Various software allows administrators to track performance, detect issues, and optimize operations.

Monitoring Tools

Tools like Nagios, Zabbix, and Grafana can help you monitor system metrics.

Example 6: Setting Up Nagios for Monitoring

1. **Install Nagios:**

   - Follow installation guidelines specific to your operating system (e.g., for CentOS, use `yum install nagios`).

2. **Configure Nagios:**

   - Edit the `nagios.cfg` configuration file to define the host and service you want to monitor.

3. **Add Hosts:**

   - Create a new configuration file in `/etc/nagios/conf.d/`, where you define your hosts' parameters.

4. **Launch Nagios Web Interface:**

   - Access it through your web browser at `http://your-server-ip/nagios`. Log in using your defined credentials.

5. **Check for Alerts:**

   - Set up email notifications to receive alerts when systems are down or performance metrics are exceeded.

Management Tools

Configuration management tools like Ansible,

Puppet, or Chef help automate the process of managing and configuring systems.

Example 7: Automating with Ansible

1. **Install Ansible:**

   - Use `apt-get install ansible` on Debian-based distros or `yum install ansible` for Red Hat-based distros.

2. **Define Your Inventory:**

   - Create a file called `hosts` where you list all your managed nodes.

3. **Write Playbooks:**

   - Create a YAML file (`deploy.yml`) containing the steps you want to automate:

   ```yaml
   - hosts: all

     tasks:
   ```

```
- name: Install Apache

  become: yes

  apt:

    name: apache2

    state: present
```
```

4. **Run Your Playbook:**

   - Execute the command `ansible-playbook -i hosts deploy.yml`, and Ansible will install Apache on all specified hosts.


## 4.4. Backup and Recovery


Data loss can occur due to various reasons, from hardware failure to accidental deletions. A comprehensive backup strategy ensures data integrity and availability.


### Backup Strategies
```

An effective backup strategy incorporates full, incremental, and differential backups.

Example 8: Setting Up a Backup Schedule in Windows

1. **Open Backup and Restore:**

   - Go to `Control Panel` > `System and Security` > `Backup and Restore`.

2. **Set Up Backup:**

   - Click on `Set up backup` and choose your backup location (either an external drive or network location).

3. **Select What to Backup:**

   - Choose `Let Windows choose` or `Let me choose` for specific folders/files.

4. **Schedule Backup:**

   - Set the frequency for backups (e.g., daily, weekly) and click `Save Settings and Run Backup`.

Data Recovery

Data recovery tools can aid in the restoration of data from backups.

Example 9: Restoring Files from Backup in Linux

1. **Identify Backup Location:**

   - Make sure you know where your backup files are stored (e.g., a dedicated backup server or external storage).

2. **Use `rsync` for Restoration:**

   - Utilize the Rsync command to restore files:

```bash

rsync -av --progress /backup/location /original/location

```

3. **Verify Restored Files:**

   - Check the integrity of restored files by comparing checksums before and after restoration using `md5sum`.

4. **Regular Test Restores:**

   - Schedule regular test restores to ensure your backup works as intended.

In summary, mastering these tools and technologies is crucial for System Administrators. Operating systems, virtualization technologies, monitoring tools, and effective backup strategies provide you with the capability to maintain a stable and efficient IT environment. By continuously learning and adapting these practices, you'll ensure that you are well-equipped to handle the challenges of system administration.

Chapter 5: Network Management

5.1. Networking Fundamentals

Networking is an essential aspect of system administration, involving the connection of computers and devices to share resources and communicate. Understanding networking fundamentals is crucial for administrators to efficiently manage and troubleshoot networks.

1. Networking Concepts:

   - **Definition of a Network:** A network comprises computers and devices interconnected to share resources such as files, applications, and internet connectivity.

   - **Types of Networks:**

      - **LAN (Local Area Network):** Covers a small geographical area, such as a single building.

      - **WAN (Wide Area Network):** Covers a large geographical area, often consisting of multiple LANs.

   - **MAN (Metropolitan Area Network):** A network that spans a city or large campus.

   - **PAN (Personal Area Network):** A small network for personal devices, typically within a range of a few meters.

2. Network Topologies:

   - **Star Topology:** All devices connect to a central hub.

   - **Bus Topology:** All devices share a single communication line.

   - **Ring Topology:** Each device connects to two others, forming a ring.

   - **Mesh Topology:** Each device connects to multiple others, providing various paths for data.

3. Network Devices:

   - **Router:** A device that forwards data packets between networks.

- **Switch:** A device that connects devices within a LAN and uses MAC addresses to forward data.

- **Access Point:** A device that allows wireless devices to connect to a wired network.

- **Modem:** A device that modulates and demodulates signals for internet connectivity.

4. OSI Model:

- The **Open Systems Interconnection (OSI)** model consists of seven layers:

1. **Physical Layer:** Deals with the physical connection and transmission of data.

2. **Data Link Layer:** Manages node-to-node data transfer and error detection.

3. **Network Layer:** Determines how data is sent between devices on a network.

4. **Transport Layer:** Manages end-to-end communication and error recovery.

5. **Session Layer:** Manages sessions in which data is transferred.

6. **Presentation Layer:** Translates data formats and encrypts data.

7. **Application Layer:** Interfaces with the end-user applications.

5. Network Protocols:

- Protocols are rules that govern data communication.

- Common protocols include:

  - **HTTP/HTTPS:** Used for web traffic.

  - **FTP/SFTP:** Used for file transfers.

  - **SMTP/IMAP:** Used for email communication.

  - **Telnet/SSH:** Used for remote administrative access.

5.2. Configuring Routers and Switches

Configuring routers and switches involves setting them up to manage network traffic effectively. Here's a step-by-step guide on how to configure a basic router and switch using a command-line interface.

Configuring a Router

Example: Basic Router Configuration:

1. **Access the Router:**

   - Connect your PC to the router's console port using a serial cable.

   - Open a terminal emulator (e.g., PuTTY or Tera Term) and set the correct COM port with settings (e.g., 9600 bps).

2. **Enter Privileged EXEC Mode:**
   ```

   Router> enable

   Router#

   ```

3. **Enter Global Configuration Mode:**

```
```

Router# configure terminal

Router(config)#

```
```

4. **Set the Hostname:**

```
```

Router(config)# hostname MyRouter

MyRouter(config)#

```
```

5. **Configure an Interface:**

   - Assign IP address to the FastEthernet interface:

```
```

   MyRouter(config)# interface fastethernet 0/0

MyRouter(config-if)# ip address
192.168.1.1 255.255.255.0

MyRouter(config-if)# no shutdown

MyRouter(config-if)# exit

```
```

6. **Configure a Default Gateway:**

```
```

MyRouter(config)# ip route 0.0.0.0 0.0.0.0
192.168.1.254

```
```

7. **Save Configuration:**

```
```

MyRouter# write memory

```
```

8. **Verify Configuration:**

```
```

MyRouter# show ip interface brief

```
```

Configuring a Switch

Example: Basic Switch Configuration:

1. **Access the Switch:**

   - Connect your PC to the switch's console port using a serial cable.

   - Launch a terminal emulator.

2. **Enter Privileged EXEC Mode:**

   ```

   Switch> enable

   Switch#

   ```

3. **Enter Global Configuration Mode:**

```
```

Switch# configure terminal

Switch(config)#

```
```

4. **Set the Hostname:**

```
```

Switch(config)# hostname MySwitch

MySwitch(config)#

```
```

5. **Configure VLANs:**

- Create a new VLAN and assign it an IP address:

```
```

MySwitch(config)# vlan 10

MySwitch(config-vlan)# name Sales

MySwitch(config-vlan)# exit

MySwitch(config)# interface vlan 10

MySwitch(config-if)# ip address
192.168.1.2 255.255.255.0

MySwitch(config-if)# no shutdown

```

6. **Assign Ports to VLAN:**

```

MySwitch(config)# interface range
fastethernet 0/1 - 24

MySwitch(config-if-range)# switchport
mode access

MySwitch(config-if-range)# switchport
access vlan 10

MySwitch(config-if-range)# exit

```

7. **Save Configuration:**
```

```
```

MySwitch# write memory

```
```

8. **Verify Configuration:**

```
```

MySwitch# show vlan brief

```
```

5.3. TCP/IP Protocol and Subnetting

Understanding TCP/IP

1. TCP/IP Model:

   - The Transmission Control Protocol/Internet Protocol (TCP/IP) model is a simpler, four-layer model compared to the OSI model:

   - **Link Layer:** Deals with the physical

and data link layers.

- **Internet Layer:** Handles packet forwarding.

- **Transport Layer:** Manages end-to-end communication through TCP or UDP.

- **Application Layer:** Corresponds to the OSI Application, Presentation, and Session layers.

2. IP Addressing:

- An IP address is a unique identifier for a device on a network.

- **IPv4 vs. IPv6:**

- IPv4 uses 32-bit addresses (e.g., 192.168.1.1).

- IPv6 uses 128-bit addresses for a larger address space (e.g., 2001:0db8:85a3:0000:0000:8a2e:0370:7334).

Subnetting

Subnetting is the process of dividing a network into smaller, manageable pieces (subnets). This practice enhances performance and increases security.

1. **Understanding Subnets:**

   - A subnet mask defines the range of IP addresses within a subnet.

   - Common subnet masks include:

     - **255.255.255.0 (Class C)**

     - **255.255.0.0 (Class B)**

     - **255.0.0.0 (Class A)**

2. **Calculating Subnets:**

   - To determine the number of subnets:

     - Formula: **2^n** (where n is the number of bits borrowed for subnetting).

   - To determine the number of hosts per subnet:

     - Formula: **$(2^h) - 2$** (where h is the

number of bits remaining for hosts).

Example of Subnetting:

Assume a Class C network: **192.168.1.0/24**

1. **Borrowing 2 Bits for Subnetting:**

   - New subnet mask: **255.255.255.252 (/30)**

   - Number of subnets: **2^2 = 4 subnets**

   - Number of hosts per subnet: **$(2^2) - 2$ = 2 hosts**

2. **Subnetting Breakdown:**

   - **Subnet 1:** 192.168.1.0 - 192.168.1.1

   - **Subnet 2:** 192.168.1.2 - 192.168.1.3

   - **Subnet 3:** 192.168.1.4 - 192.168.1.5

   - **Subnet 4:** 192.168.1.6 - 192.168.1.7

5.4. Virtual LAN (VLAN) and VPN

Virtual LAN (VLAN)

1. Overview of VLANs:

  - A **Virtual Local Area Network (VLAN)** allows the segmentation of a physical network into multiple logical networks.

  - VLANs improve security and reduce broadcast traffic.

2. Configuring VLANs:

  - VLANs are configured on switches.

  - Each VLAN has a unique identifier (ID) and can contain different devices across the physical network.

Example of VLAN Configuration:

1. Create and Assign VLANs:

```
Switch(config)# vlan 20

Switch(config-vlan)# name HR

Switch(config-vlan)# exit
```

2. Assign Ports to VLANs:

```
Switch(config)# interface fastethernet 0/5

Switch(config-if)# switchport mode access

Switch(config-if)# switchport access vlan 20

Switch(config-if)# exit
```

Virtual Private Network (VPN)

1. Overview of VPNs:

   - A **Virtual Private Network (VPN)**

creates a secure connection over the internet, allowing remote users to access a private network.

- VPNs use tunneling protocols to transmit data securely across the internet.

2. Types of VPNs:

- **Remote Access VPN:** Allows individual users to connect to a private network.

- **Site-to-Site VPN:** Connects entire networks to each other.

3. Setting Up a VPN:

Step-by-step configuration example:

1. **Choose a VPN Protocol:**

- Common protocols include IPSec, L2TP, and OpenVPN.

2. **Install VPN Software:**

   - Install VPN software on server. For example, using OpenVPN on Ubuntu:

   ```
   sudo apt-get install openvpn
   ```

3. **Configure VPN Settings:**

   - Create a configuration file for the server (e.g., `server.ovpn`).

   ```text
   port 1194

   proto udp

   dev tun

   ca ca.crt

   cert server.crt

   key server.key

   dh dh.pem
   ```

server 10.8.0.0 255.255.255.0

ifconfig-pool-persist ipp.txt

push "redirect-gateway def1 bypass-dhcp"

```
```

4. **Start the VPN Service:**

   - Start the OpenVPN service.

   ```

   sudo systemctl start openvpn@server

   ```

5. **Connect Clients:**

   - Clients will need the `.ovpn` configuration file to connect to the VPN.

6. **Testing the VPN Connection:**

   - Use a ping command to check connectivity to resources on the private network.

By understanding and implementing various networking concepts, configurations, and technologies, system administrators can effectively manage networks, optimize performance, and ensure the security and reliability of data communication. This chapter provides a foundational overview of network management essential for every system administrator.

Chapter 6: Cybersecurity

In the landscape of modern computing, cybersecurity has risen to prominence as a critical area of focus for system administrators. A robust cybersecurity posture is essential for protecting sensitive information and ensuring the integrity and availability of systems. This chapter delves into the key components of cybersecurity, providing practical step-by-step examples to illustrate the concepts outlined.

6.1. Principles of Security and Best Practices

The first step in securing an organization's data and systems is to understand the foundational principles of cybersecurity. These principles—often referred to as the "CIA Triad"—are Confidentiality, Integrity, and Availability.

6.1.1. Confidentiality

Confidentiality ensures that sensitive data is only accessible to those authorized to view it. Methods to maintain confidentiality include:

1. **User Authentication**: Implement strong authentication mechanisms like multi-factor authentication (MFA).

   - **Example**: Configure MFA for sensitive application access.

     - Step 1: Access the application settings.

     - Step 2: Enable MFA by selecting options for SMS or authenticator app prompts.

     - Step 3: Instruct users to register their devices by scanning a QR code.

2. **Access Control**: Implement role-based access control (RBAC).

   - **Example**: Assign permissions using RBAC.

- Step 1: Define roles (Administrator, User, Guest).

- Step 2: Assign permissions based on least privilege principle.

- Step 3: Regularly audit permissions to ensure compliance.

6.1.2. Integrity

Integrity guarantees that data remains accurate and unaltered unless modified by authorized users.

- **Data Validation**: Apply checks to ensure data is inputted correctly.

  - **Example**: Implement input validation in a web form.

  - Step 1: Use server-side validation to sanitize input fields.

  - Step 2: Reject any inputs that do not meet the required format.

- **Checksums and Hashes**: Utilize cryptographic hash functions to maintain data integrity.

  - **Example**: Calculate a hash for a file before and after transfer.

    - Step 1: Use a hashing algorithm (e.g., SHA-256) to compute the hash.

    - Step 2: Compare the hash pre- and post-transfer to detect modifications.

6.1.3. Availability

Availability ensures that information and resources are accessible to authorized users when needed.

- **Redundancy**: Implement systems in a redundant configuration.

  - **Example**: Use RAID for disk redundancy.

    - Step 1: Choose the RAID level (e.g.,

RAID 1 for mirroring).

   - Step 2: Set up additional drives and configure RAID in the system BIOS.

- **Regular Backups**: Schedule consistent data backups.

  - **Example**: Automate daily backups using a backup software.

   - Step 1: Select a backup solution and configure backup jobs.

   - Step 2: Store backups in multiple locations (e.g., on-premises and cloud).

6.1.4. Best Practices

- **Security Policies**: Develop and enforce clear security policies.

- **User Training**: Conduct regular training sessions to educate staff on security awareness.

- **Incident Response Plan**: Establish and

test an incident response plan.

6.2. Firewalls and Intrusion Prevention Systems (IPS)

Firewalls and IPS are critical components of network security, controlling incoming and outgoing traffic based on predefined security rules.

6.2.1. Firewalls

A firewall acts as a barrier between trusted internal networks and untrusted external networks.

- **Types of Firewalls**: Understand different firewall types (hardware, software, network-based).

- **Configuration Example**: Setting up a

simple enterprise firewall (using pfSense):

- Step 1: Install pfSense on compatible hardware.

- Step 2: Access the web interface and login.

- Step 3: Configure WAN and LAN interfaces with appropriate IP addresses.

- Step 4: Create firewall rules (e.g., block all incoming traffic except for HTTP/HTTPS).

6.2.2. Intrusion Prevention Systems (IPS)

An IPS monitors network and/or system activities for malicious activity.

- **Deployment Example**: Implementing Snort as an IDS/IPS:

- Step 1: Install Snort on a server.

- Step 2: Configure Snort by editing the `snort.conf` file to define network variables and rules.

- Step 3: Enable packet logging and alerting.

- Step 4: Integrate Snort with a SIEM (Security Information and Event Management) tool for real-time monitoring.

6.2.3. Regular Updates and Monitoring

- Regularly update firewall and IPS rules to defend against new threats.

- Monitor logs for unusual activity and establish alerts for critical events.

6.3. Vulnerability Management and Patch Management

Vulnerability management refers to identifying, evaluating, treating, and reporting on security vulnerabilities in systems and software.

6.3.1. Vulnerability Scanning

Regular vulnerability scanning can proactively identify weaknesses in systems.

- **Using OpenVAS for Scanning**:

  - Step 1: Install OpenVAS according to your distribution's guidelines.

  - Step 2: Run a setup command to configure the scanner.

  - Step 3: Schedule regular scans on critical systems and review reports.

6.3.2. Patch Management

Timely patching of systems is critical for maintaining security.

- **Patch Management Process**:

  - **Assessment**: Regularly assess systems for patches.

- Step 1: Use tools like WSUS for Windows or Unattended Upgrades for Linux.

- **Deployment**: Test and deploy patches to production systems.

    - Step 2: Create a testing environment for patches.

    - Step 3: Monitor systems post-deployment for issues.

- **Documentation**: Keep detailed records of applied patches.

    - Step 4: Use a Management Information System (MIS) to track patches.

6.4. Data Protection and Cryptography

Data protection involves implementing measures to safeguard sensitive information from unauthorized access and breaches.

6.4.1. Data Encryption

Encryption is the cornerstone of data protection, ensuring that even if data is intercepted, it remains unreadable.

- **Example of Implementing Full Disk Encryption**:

  - **On Windows (BitLocker)**:

    - Step 1: Access Control Panel and navigate to BitLocker Drive Encryption.

    - Step 2: Enable BitLocker for the desired drive and choose an authentication method (e.g., password or smart card).

  - **On Linux (LUKS)**:

    - Step 3: Use `cryptsetup` to configure LUKS on the drive:

      ```bash
      sudo cryptsetup luksFormat /dev/sdaX
      ```

```
    sudo cryptsetup luksOpen /dev/sdaX
my_encrypted_drive

    mkfs.ext4
/dev/mapper/my_encrypted_drive

    ```
```

6.4.2. Data Backup and Recovery Planning

Data protection also encompasses strategies for backup and recovery.

- **Backup Strategies with Encryption**:

  - Step 1: Choose backup software that supports encryption (e.g., Veeam, Acronis).

  - Step 2: Configure encrypted backups and ensure that encryption keys are securely stored.

- **Testing Recovery Processes**:
```

- Step 3: Regularly test data recovery processes to ensure they function as intended.

6.4.3. Secure Communication

Utilize encryption protocols (TLS, SSH) to secure data in transit.

- **Implementing HTTPS**:

  - Step 1: Obtain an SSL certificate from a Certificate Authority (CA).

  - Step 2: Configure your web server (Apache, Nginx) to use HTTPS.

  - **Example Configuration for Nginx**:
    ```nginx
    server {
        listen 443 ssl;
        ssl_certificate /etc/ssl/certs/your_domain.crt;
    ```

```
    ssl_certificate_key
/etc/ssl/private/your_domain.key;

    ...

}

```
```

In conclusion, the role of a system administrator in the realm of cybersecurity is multifaceted and requires a comprehensive understanding of various principles, practices, and tools. By establishing a strong foundation in the principles of confidentiality, integrity, and availability, implementing firewalls and intrusion prevention mechanisms, managing vulnerabilities and patches effectively, and utilizing data protection strategies—including encryption—system administrators can significantly mitigate risks. The examples illustrated in this chapter offer practical insights into the implementation of these concepts, providing a roadmap for creating a secure computing environment. As threats continue to evolve, ongoing education and adaptation are critical components of a successful cybersecurity strategy.
```

Chapter 7: System Administration

In this chapter, we will explore several key aspects of system administration, including server configuration and management, user management and permissions, task automation, and system performance monitoring. Each section will provide practical steps and examples to help you grasp these concepts clearly.

7.1 Configuring and Managing Servers

7.1.1 Understanding Server Types

Before we dive into server configuration, it's essential to understand the types of servers commonly used in a network environment:

- **Web Servers**: Host websites and serve web pages to users. Popular web servers include Apache and Nginx.

- **Database Servers**: Store and manage databases. Common examples include MySQL, PostgreSQL, and Microsoft SQL Server.

- **File Servers**: Store files and allow users to access and share them over a network. Solutions can vary from Windows File Server to Samba on Linux.

- **Application Servers**: Host applications and deliver web applications to users. Examples include JBoss and GlassFish.

7.1.2 Step-by-Step Server Configuration Example

Let's go through the process of configuring a web server using Apache on an Ubuntu server.

Step 1: Install Apache

First, log in to your server via SSH and update the package manager:

```bash
sudo apt update
sudo apt upgrade
```

Then, install Apache with the following command:

```bash
sudo apt install apache2
```

Step 2: Start and Enable Apache Service

To ensure that the Apache service starts automatically at boot, run:

```bash
```

```
sudo systemctl start apache2

sudo systemctl enable apache2

```
```

Step 3: Adjust Firewall Settings

If you are using UFW (Uncomplicated Firewall), allow HTTP and HTTPS traffic:

```bash
sudo ufw allow 'Apache Full'
```

Step 4: Test the Installation

To verify that Apache is working correctly, open a web browser and navigate to your server's IP address. If everything is set up properly, you should see the Apache default page.
```

Step 5: Configure Virtual Hosts

To host multiple websites on a single server, you can set up virtual hosts. Create a new configuration file for your site:

```bash
sudo nano /etc/apache2/sites-available/example.com.conf
```

Add the following configuration:

```apache
<VirtualHost *:80>
    ServerName example.com
    ServerAlias www.example.com
    DocumentRoot /var/www/example.com/public_html
```

    ErrorLog $
{APACHE_LOG_DIR}/error.log

    CustomLog $
{APACHE_LOG_DIR}/access.log combined

</VirtualHost>

```

#### Step 6: Enable the New Virtual Host

Enable the new site and reload Apache for the changes to take effect:

```bash

sudo a2ensite example.com.conf

sudo systemctl reload apache2

```

7.1.3 Basic Server Management
```

After configuring your server, it's crucial to manage it effectively. Here are some basic management tasks:

- **Backup**: Regularly backup server data. Use tools like `rs

Chapter 8: Project Management

Project management is a critical skill for a system administrator, particularly in environments where technology plays an essential role in business operations. Effective project management ensures that projects are delivered on time, within budget, and to the satisfaction of stakeholders. In this chapter, we will explore project management methodologies, tools, and the importance of documentation and reporting.

8.1 Project Management Methodologies

Understanding project management methodologies is crucial for successfully running projects. Two commonly used methodologies are Agile and Waterfall.

8.1.1 Agile Methodology

Agile is an iterative project management methodology that promotes flexibility and collaboration. It's especially beneficial when project requirements are likely to change or evolve. Here's a step-by-step example of applying Agile principles to a system administration project, such as migrating a legacy system to cloud infrastructure.

Step 1: Define the Project Scope

Before starting the migration, gather the team to outline the project's scope. Identify key stakeholders, project goals, and the requirements for a successful migration. Create a product backlog that includes all necessary tasks like planning, testing, and deployment.

Step 2: Organize the Team

Assign roles within the team, including a Scrum Master, Product Owner, and

Development Team members. The Scrum
Master facilitates the process, while the
Product Owner keeps the backlog prioritized
based on stakeholder input.

Step 3: Plan Sprints

Organize the project into sprints, typically
lasting 2-4 weeks. Each sprint will focus on
specific tasks from the product backlog. For
instance, in Sprint 1, you might tackle setting
up a staging environment in the cloud, while
Sprint 2 might focus on migrating database
services.

Step 4: Daily Stand-ups

Hold daily stand-up meetings to discuss
progress, impediments, and goals for the day.
This consistent communication helps identify
challenges quickly and keeps the project
moving forward.

Step 5: Review and Retrospect

At the end of each sprint, conduct a sprint review to demonstrate completed work to stakeholders and gather their feedback. Follow this with a retrospective meeting to assess what went well, what needs improvement, and how the next sprint can be enhanced.

8.1.2 Waterfall Methodology

Waterfall is a linear and sequential approach to project management that is suited for projects with well-defined requirements. Here's how to implement the Waterfall method in a project, like upgrading network infrastructure.

Step 1: Requirements Analysis

Gather requirements through meetings with stakeholders. Document the technical specifications necessary for the upgrade, including hardware and software requirements.

Step 2: System Design

Create a detailed design plan based on the gathered requirements. This phase should include network diagrams, specifications for new devices, and a timeline for completion.

Step 3: Implementation

Execute the plan as designed. For example, replace old routers and switches with new ones according to the schedule laid out in the design phase. Each step should be completed before moving onto the next.

Step 4: Verification

After implementation, conduct thorough testing to ensure the upgrade meets the initial requirements. This includes verifying that the network is stable, secure, and scalable.

Step 5: Maintenance

Once the project is complete and verified, shift focus to ongoing maintenance, ensuring that the upgraded infrastructure operates smoothly.

8.1.3 Choosing the Right Methodology

Deciding whether to use Agile or Waterfall depends on the project's nature, its requirements, and the organizational context. Agile is preferable for projects with evolving requirements, while Waterfall suits projects with clear, unchanging specifications.

8.2 Utilizing Project Management Tools

In today's tech landscape, various tools can assist system administrators in managing projects effectively. Some popular project management tools include Trello, JIRA, Asana, and Microsoft Project.

8.2.1 Trello

Trello is a visual project management tool based on Kanban boards. It allows a team to handle tasks using cards that can be moved between different columns representing task statuses (e.g., To Do, In Progress, Done).

Step-by-Step Example of Using Trello

1. **Create a Board**: Set up a new board named "Infrastructure Upgrade Project".

2. **Create Lists**: Add lists such as

"Backlog," "To Do," "In Progress," "In Review," and "Completed".

3. **Add Cards**: For each task identified in the project scope, create a card. For example, "Install new routers" and "Configure firewall settings."

4. **Assign Tasks**: Assign team members to each card to clarify responsibility.

5. **Customize Cards**: Attach documents, due dates, and checklists to cards to track the progress of each task.

6. **Monitor Progress**: Regularly check the board to monitor statuses, moving cards accordingly as tasks progress.

8.2.2 JIRA

JIRA is primarily used for Agile project management, offering powerful tracking and reporting features.

Step-by-Step Example of Using JIRA

1. **Create a Project**: Set up a new project in JIRA, selecting the Scrum template.

2. **Create User Stories**: Input user stories based on your product backlog, such as "As a user, I want to log in securely."

3. **Plan Sprints**: Use the sprint planning module to set a sprint duration and select stories to work on during that time.

4. **Track Progress**: Utilize the burndown chart to monitor sprint progress and adjust task priorities as needed.

5. **Conduct Sprint Reviews**: After the sprint, review completed work in the sprint review meeting and capture feedback in JIRA for future iterations.

8.2.3 Microsoft Project

Microsoft Project is a versatile tool for managing tasks, budgets, and timelines.

Step-by-Step Example of Using Microsoft Project

1. **Create a New Project**: Open Microsoft Project and start a new project.

2. **Define Tasks**: Input all tasks identified for your project, including dependencies and durations.

3. **Assign Resources**: Assign team members to tasks, indicating their availability and workloads.

4. **Set Milestones**: Create milestones to represent critical points in the project timeline, such as completion of the main upgrade.

5. **Generate Reports**: Use in-built reporting tools to track project progress and resource allocation, adjusting tasks as necessary.

8.3 Documentation and Reporting

Good documentation and reporting are vital

components of successful project management. They ensure transparency, provide reference material for future projects, and enhance communication among stakeholders.

8.3.1 Documentation Types

1. **Project Charter**: A document that outlines the project's purpose, objectives, stakeholders, and overall scope.

2. **Requirements Document**: Detailed specifications outlining project requirements.

3. **Design Document**: This covers the architecture and design of the project implementation.

4. **Test Plans and Results**: Documentation of how testing will be performed and the results of those tests.

5. **User Manuals**: Guides for end-users detailing how to utilize new systems or tools.

6. **Post-Implementation Review**: A report evaluating the project's success against its

objectives, complete with lessons learned.

8.3.2 Effective Reporting

1. **Status Reports**: Regularly provide stakeholders with updates on project progress, risks, and issues.

2. **Performance Metrics**: Use key performance indicators (KPIs) to measure project success (e.g., adherence to schedule, budget).

3. **Change Logs**: Maintain a record of changes in project scope, requirements, or resources, including reasons for changes.

Step-by-Step Example of Creating Documentation for a Migration Project

1. **Start with a Project Charter**: Outline the purpose of migrating to the cloud, its objectives, key stakeholders, and high-level timelines.

2. **Gather Requirements**: Conduct

meetings with stakeholders to document functional and non-functional requirements.

3. **Create a Design Document**: Draft a document detailing the network architecture and services to be migrated.

4. **Develop a Test Plan**: Outline your approach for testing each component of the migration to validate its performance post-migration.

5. **Compile a User Manual**: Provide step-by-step instructions for end-users on accessing and utilizing the new cloud services.

6. **Conduct a Post-Implementation Review**: After the migration, meet with stakeholders to evaluate the project's success, documenting lessons learned for future reference.

Successful project management is vital for system administrators, encompassing the choice of methodology, the use of effective tools, and a commitment to clear documentation and reporting. By mastering these components, administrators can significantly enhance their project delivery, satisfaction, and overall team effectiveness.

Chapter 9: Soft Skills and Communication

In today's rapidly evolving technological landscape, the role of a System Administrator (SysAdmin) extends far beyond the mere technicalities of managing systems and networks. As crucial as it is to possess robust technical skills, the importance of soft skills cannot be underestimated. This chapter will delve deep into the essential soft skills required for successful System Administrators, focusing on effective communication, collaborative teamwork, and adept problem-solving capabilities alongside stress management.

9.1 Importance of Soft Skills for a System Administrator

Soft skills refer to the interpersonal attributes and communication abilities that enable individuals to interact effectively with others. For System Administrators, these skills are vital in fostering teamwork, building relationships with clients, and navigating the complexities of organizational dynamics.

Key Soft Skills for System Administrators

1. **Communication Skills**: System Administrators often find themselves in situations where they need to explain technical concepts to non-technical stakeholders. The ability to communicate effectively is fundamental.

   Example: An Administrator must explain why a system update is necessary to a department head who may have little understanding of IT. Instead of using jargon, an effective description might involve outlining the benefits, such as enhanced security, increased speed, and reduced downtime.

2. **Team Collaboration**: Working as part

of a team is often inevitable, especially when dealing with larger projects. Collaborative skills involve cooperation, understanding, and appreciation of others' roles and contributions.

   Example: A System Administrator is part of a project team implementing a new software solution. They must collaborate with developers, quality assurance testers, and business analysts. Regular check-ins and updates on project status and mutual assistance establish a collaborative environment.

3. **Problem-Solving**: The ability to analyze issues, come up with effective solutions, and implement those solutions is crucial, especially under pressure.

   Example: If a server goes down unexpectedly, a System Administrator quickly assesses the situation, determining whether the issue is hardware or software-related. They then either restore operations through a backup solution or coordinate with the hardware vendor for replacement parts.

4. **Adaptability**: The technology landscape can change rapidly, and an effective Administrator must be willing to adapt to new tools, processes, and organizational changes.

   Example: If the company decides to migrate to a new cloud service, the SysAdmin must quickly learn the new platform's intricacies and train their team on its use.

5. **Emotional Intelligence**: This involves understanding one's own emotions and those of others, assisting in managing relationships thoughtfully and empathetically.

   Example: A SysAdmin encounters a team member frustrated with technological issues. Displaying emotional intelligence, they listen to the colleague's concerns and offer assistance while remaining calm under pressure.

9.2 Effective Communication with Teams and Clients

Effective communication is the backbone of successful System Administration. Let's explore key strategies for improving communication with both internal teams and external clients.

Strategies for Effective Team Communication

1. **Regular Updates and Meetings**: Keeping the team informed about ongoing projects and changes ensures everyone is on the same page.

   Example: Weekly stand-up meetings can help each team member share their progress, discuss roadblocks, and outline next steps. Utilizing a shared platform, like Slack or Microsoft Teams, for ongoing updates fosters a collaborative environment.

2. **Utilization of Clear Language**: Avoiding technical jargon when communicating with non-tech colleagues is essential to ensure understanding.

   Example: When explaining the necessity of a firewall update, a SysAdmin might say, "This update protects our systems from cyber threats, which can compromise sensitive data and disrupt our operations" instead of "This patch addresses vulnerabilities in the firmware."

3. **Active Listening**: Engaging in active listening means fully focusing on the speaker, understanding their message, responding thoughtfully, and retaining what's being said.

   Example: During a meeting, if a team

member raises a concern about server load, an effective SysAdmin should acknowledge this by asking follow-up questions to dig deeper into the issue rather than immediately jumping into possible solutions.

4. **Feedback Mechanisms**: Encouraging and providing constructive feedback can greatly enhance team dynamics and project outcomes.

   Example: After completing a project, conducting a retrospective meeting where everyone can share what went well and what could be improved allows for continuous learning and growth.

Communicating with Clients

1. **Understanding Client Needs**: It's crucial to identify and understand the specific needs and concerns of clients. This can be achieved through effective questioning and

active listening.

Example: When onboarding a new client, a SysAdmin might conduct a structured interview to uncover their primary concerns and expectations regarding system performance and security.

2. **Establishing Trust**: Building a trusting relationship with clients ensures that they feel comfortable discussing their concerns and requirements.

Example: Sharing successful case studies or testimonials from past clients can effectively establish credibility and trust early in the relationship.

3. **Providing Transparent Updates**: Keeping clients updated about any changes, challenges, or delays in service is essential for maintaining transparency.

Example: If a system will be down for maintenance, a SysAdmin should communicate this well in advance, providing details on the duration and expected impact on the client's operations.

4. **Follow-up After Support**: Checking in after a support request to ensure the issue was resolved to the client's satisfaction is a critical step in relationship-building.

Example: After resolving a technical issue for a client, the SysAdmin might send a brief email asking if the client has any further questions and if everything is running smoothly. This indicates care and commitment to service.

9.3 Problem Solving and Stress Management

In the demanding environment of IT systems administration, problem-solving skills and the ability to manage stress are crucial for maintaining operational effectiveness.

Problem-Solving Steps

1. **Identify the Problem**: Quickly assessing the situation to identify the root cause is the first step to effective problem-solving.

   Example: After receiving multiple reports of slow network performance, a SysAdmin should first check server logs, network traffic, and endpoint connectivity to determine if there's a bottleneck.

2. **Evaluate Possible Solutions**: Once the problem is identified, the next step is to brainstorm potential solutions, weighing their pros and cons.

   Example: If the root cause is

determined to be insufficient bandwidth, the SysAdmin might consider options such as upgrading the bandwidth, optimizing existing load, or deploying additional caching mechanisms.

3. **Implement the Chosen Solution**: After selective evaluation, the chosen solution must be executed carefully to minimize disruption.

   Example: Implementing a bandwidth upgrade during off-peak hours to ensure minimal impact on users.

4. **Monitor Results**: Post-implementation, it is essential to monitor the results to ensure the problem has been resolved effectively.

   Example: Following the bandwidth upgrade, the SysAdmin should track network performance over the next few weeks to confirm improvements and identify any new issues.

5. **Document the Process**: Keeping a record of issue resolution processes provides valuable reference data for future similar problems.

   Example: Creating a detailed incident report that includes symptoms, identification, solution, and outcome helps in establishing a knowledge base.

Stress Management Techniques

1. **Time Management**: Prioritizing tasks based on urgency and importance helps in managing workload and reduces stress.

   Example: Using tools like the Eisenhower Matrix can help distinguish between what is urgent and what is important, allowing for more focus and less overwhelm.

2. **Taking Breaks**: Regular breaks during a hectic workday help recharge mental capacity.

   Example: A SysAdmin might implement the Pomodoro Technique—a method of working in focused bursts of 25 minutes followed by a 5-minute break—to maintain productivity and reduce burnout.

3. **Seeking Support**: Having a support network, whether through colleagues or professional networks, can provide an outlet for discussing challenges and solutions.

   Example: Joining an online forum or community where System Administrators share experiences and advice helps to relieve stress and gain new insights.

4. **Mindfulness and Relaxation Techniques**: Engaging in mindfulness exercises can significantly alleviate stress and

improve focus.

Example: Practicing mindfulness meditation for just a few minutes a day can enhance mental clarity and emotional regulation, which are essential when dealing with high-pressure situations in IT.

5. **Work-Life Balance**: Ensuring a healthy work-life balance is crucial to long-term success and reduces burnout.

Example: Setting clear boundaries around work hours helps in separating professional responsibilities from personal time, allowing for rejuvenation and better performance when at work.

Conclusion

In conclusion, the integration of soft skills—particularly effective communication, problem-solving, and stress management—is essential for a successful System Administrator. In an increasingly collaborative and complex digital workplace, these skills enable SysAdmins not only to solve problems effectively but also to interact positively with team members and clients. By developing these interpersonal skills, System Administrators can enhance their professional development and contribute to a more harmonious and productive work environment. Ultimately, the ability to balance technical expertise with strong interpersonal skills is what distinguishes a good System Administrator from a great one.

Chapter 10: Case Studies and Practical Scenarios

In this chapter, we will delve into real-world scenarios that a System Administrator may encounter. The focus will be on three crucial areas: **Configuration of Corporate Networks**, **Incident Management and Common Issues**, and **System Migration and Upgrades**. Through step-by-step examples, we will illustrate the complexities and best practices involved in each area.

10.1. Examples of Corporate Network Configuration

Scenario: Configuring a Basic Corporate Network

Objective: Set up a network for a medium-sized organization consisting of 50 employees, ensuring that the network is efficient, secure, and scalable.

Tools Required:

- Router

- Switch (24-port managed switch)

- Access Points (three for wireless connectivity)

- Network cables (CAT6)

- Firewall (hardware-based)

- Network Attached Storage (NAS)

- Workstations (50 PCs)

- Server (for hosting applications and files)

- DHCP server (often integrated into routers)

- Static IP address documentation

Step 1: Planning the Network Layout

Before any configuration, design a basic layout. For our example, we'll have:

- An office environment where workstations are arranged in clusters.

- A server room located centrally to minimize cable lengths.

- Router connected to the internet.

- Switches to connect workstations.

- Access points for wireless devices like laptops and tablets.

Step 2: Setting Up the Router

1. **Connect the Router:**

   - Connect the router to the internet service provider (ISP) modem using the WAN port.

   - Connect the internal LAN port to the switch.

2. **Access the Router's Configuration Interface:**

   - Open a web browser and enter the router's IP address (commonly 192.168.1.1).

   - Log in with the default username and

password.

3. **Configure Basic Settings:**

   - Change the default admin password for security.

   - Rename the default SSID (for WiFi) to something identifiable (e.g., "Company_Network").

   - Set the DHCP range (e.g., 192.168.1.100 to 192.168.1.200) to provide IP addresses for dynamic devices.

4. **Save and Reboot the Router:**

Step 3: Setting Up the Switch

1. **Power on the Switch:**

   - Plug in the switch and connect it to the router using a CAT6 cable (from the router's LAN port to the switch).

2. **Connect Workstations:**

   - Connect each workstation to the switch using CAT6 cables.

   - Label each cable for future reference.

3. **Configure VLANs if necessary:**

   - Access the switch management interface.

   - Create VLANs to segment traffic (e.g., one for HR, one for Sales).

Step 4: Configuring Wireless Access Points

1. **Connect Access Points:**

   - Connect each access point to the switch.

2. **Access Configuration:**

   - Similar to the router, access each AP's configuration interface through a web browser using the device's IP.

3. **Set Up Wireless Security:**

   - Use WPA3 for security.

   - Set a robust password for accessing the Wi-Fi network.

   - Assign static IPs to APs for easier management.

Step 5: Implementing Network Security

1. **Install the Firewall:**

   - Place a firewall between the router and the switch.

   - Configure inbound/outbound rules to restrict unauthorized access.

2. **Regular Security Audits:**

   - Plan periodic audits of the network for vulnerabilities.

3. **User Training:**

- Conduct training sessions for employees on cybersecurity best practices.

Summary of the Network Configuration Scenario

By following the outlined steps, the organization now has a fully operational and secure corporate network capable of supporting its 50 employees. Addressing the design, security, and scalability from the outset ensures efficient network operations.

10.2. Incident Management and Common Issues

In addition to network setup, system administrators must deal with various incidents and issues. Here we will discuss common problems and how to effectively manage them.

Scenario: Network Outage Incident

Objective: Respond quickly to a network outage that impacts all employees.

Step 1: Incident Detection

1. **Identify the Problem:**

   - Employees report they cannot access the internet or internal applications.

   - Use monitoring tools like PRTG or Nagios to confirm network outages.

Step 2: Initial Troubleshooting

1. **Check Physical Connections:**

   - Ensure all network cables are firmly connected, including those from the router to the switch.

2. **Check LED Indicators:**

   - Look for warning lights on the router and switches.

   - If any critical lights (such as power, or WAN, are off), troubleshoot those devices.

Step 3: Diagnose the Cause

1. **Ping Tests:**

   - Use the command prompt to ping the router (usually 192.168.1.1).

   - If unable to reach, the issue may lie with the router.

2. **Access Router Configuration:**

   - If no physical issues are found, access the router's interface.

   - Check for any observed settings or errors notified by the device logs.

3. **Review Recent Changes:**

   - Investigate if any changes were made recently that could affect connectivity, including firewall rules or DHCP assignments.

Step 4: Resolving the Issue

1. **Reboot Hardware:**

   - Reboot the router and switches if they remain unresponsive.

2. **Evaluate ISP Issues:**

   - If connectivity persists, contact the ISP to check for outages.

3. **Document the Incident:**

   - Document the incident's timeline, actions, and resolutions for future reference and training.

Step 5: Post-Incident Review

1. **Conduct a Debrief:**

   - After resolving the issue, hold a meeting to discuss what was learned.

2. **Draft a New Incident Response Plan:**

   - Create or update procedures based on the incident to minimize downtime in the future.

Summary of Incident Management

Effective incident management involves quick identification, systematic troubleshooting, and thorough documentation for continuous improvement. Using established protocols can significantly reduce downtime.

10.3. System Migration and Upgrades

Scenario: Migrating from Old Servers to New Virtualized Environment

Objective: Transition of services from physical servers to a virtualized environment using VMware.

Step 1: Planning the Migration

1. **Assessment:**

   - Document all services running on the existing servers (e.g., databases, applications).

2. **Choose Virtualization Technology:**

   - Select between VMware, Hyper-V, or other platforms according to organizational needs.

3. **Resource Allocation:**

   - Plan the hardware requirements based on

the workloads to minimize performance hits.

Step 2: Preparation of the New Environment

1. **Install Virtualization Software:**

   - Set up ESXi on new server hardware as the hypervisor.

2. **Configure Management Interface:**

   - Set up the VMware vCenter for centralized management.

Step 3: Creating Virtual Machines

1. **Initial VM Configuration:**

   - Create VMs mirroring the specifications of the existing servers: CPU, RAM, storage.

Step 4: Data Migration

1. **Data Backup:**

   - Use backup software to back up data from the existing servers.

2. **Transfer Data:**

   - Use rsync, SCP, or third-party tools to transfer data to virtual machines.

3. **Install Applications:**

   - Set up the necessary applications on new virtual machines as per initial assessments.

Step 5: Testing the New Setup

1. **Functional Testing:**

   - Carry out extensive tests to verify that applications and services run as expected.

2. **Roll Back Plan:**

   - Maintain an option to revert to legacy servers should any issues arise during or after the migration.

Step 6: Finalizing the Migration

1. **DNS Changes:**

   - Point DNS records to the new virtual environments.

2. **Decommission Old Servers:**

   - Securely wipe old server data and consult with stakeholders for decommissioning procedures.

Summary of System Migration

A structured and methodical approach to

migration is crucial. Every step from planning to testing ensures seamless transitions and minimizes downtime and data integrity issues.

Chapter 11: Terminology Used in System Administration

In this chapter, we will delve into key terms and concepts frequently encountered in the realm of system administration. Understanding these terms is vital for effective communication, problem-solving, and managing IT infrastructure. System administrators are tasked with a variety of responsibilities, from maintaining servers and networks to troubleshooting hardware and software issues. By familiarizing ourselves with the terminology used in system administration, we can better navigate the complexities of the profession.

1. System Administration

Definition: System administration refers to the management of computer systems, servers, and networks to ensure they function efficiently and securely. This includes installation, configuration, maintenance, and troubleshooting.

Practical Example: Imagine you have been tasked with setting up a new server for your organization. As a system administrator, you would need to install the operating system, configure network settings, set up user accounts, and ensure that the server is secure and up-to-date with the latest patches.

2. Operating System (OS)

Definition: An operating system is software that manages hardware and software resources on a computer. It provides common services for computer programs.

Practical Example: When configuring a new Linux server, you might choose a distribution such as Ubuntu Server. After installing the OS, you would proceed to configure network settings, install necessary packages, and secure the server using system tools like `iptables` for firewall settings.

3. Shell

Definition: A shell is a command-line interface that allows users to interact with the operating system by typing commands.

Practical Example: When using a Linux server, you might use the Bash shell to navigate the filesystem. For instance, using the command `cd /var/www/html` will change your directory to the specified path where your web application files are stored.

4. Command Line Interface (CLI)

Definition: The CLI is a text-based interface used to interact with an operating system or application. It requires users to enter commands.

Practical Example: You can check the status of services running on a Windows server through the CLI by using the `sc query` command. For example, executing `sc query wuauserv` allows you to see the status of the Windows Update service.

5. Graphical User Interface (GUI)

Definition: A GUI is a visual way for users to interact with computer systems through graphical elements like windows, icons, and menus.

Practical Example: On a system with a Windows GUI, you can manage users and groups by accessing the "Computer Management" utility, navigating to "Local Users and Groups," and creating a new user through a wizard.

6. File System

Definition: A file system is the method and data structure that an operating system uses to manage files on a disk or storage device.

Practical Example: In Linux, the file hierarchy starts from the root directory `/`. To create a new directory for a web application, you could use the command `mkdir /var/www/html/myapp`.

7. Virtualization

Definition: Virtualization is the creation of virtual versions of physical resources, such as servers, storage devices, or network resources.

Practical Example: You may use VMware or VirtualBox to set up a virtual machine (VM) on your physical server. This allows you to run multiple operating systems on a single physical machine, which can be useful for development or testing.

8. Hypervisor

Definition: A hypervisor is software that creates and manages virtual machines by pooling physical resources.

Practical Example: If you are using KVM (Kernel-based Virtual Machine) on a Linux host, you can manage your virtual machines with tools like `virsh`. For instance, you might start a VM with the command `virsh start myvm`.

9. Backup and Recovery

Definition: Backup refers to the process of making copies of data to protect against data loss. Recovery is the process of restoring data from a backup.

Practical Example: You can use `rsync` to back up directories in Linux. The command `rsync -avz /home/user/data /backup/data` can efficiently copy your data to a backup location, preserving permissions and timestamps.

10. Active Directory (AD)

Definition: Active Directory is a directory service developed by Microsoft for Windows domain networks. It is used for managing permissions and user access to network resources.

Practical Example: To create a new user in Active Directory, you can use the Active Directory Users and Computers (ADUC) tool. After selecting the appropriate organizational unit, you can right-click and choose "New" > "User," following the wizard to set up details like username and password.

11. Network Protocol

Definition: A network protocol is a set of rules and conventions for communication between network devices.

Practical Example: The Transmission Control Protocol (TCP) is an essential protocol for reliable communication over networks, ensuring that data packets are delivered in order. You might use the command `ping` to test connectivity to another computer using its IP address, which operates over the Internet Control Message Protocol (ICMP).

12. Firewall

Definition: A firewall is a network security system that monitors and controls incoming and outgoing network traffic based on predetermined security rules.

Practical Example: In a Linux environment, you can configure `iptables` to manage firewall rules. For instance, executing `iptables -A INPUT -p tcp --dport 22 -j ACCEPT` would allow incoming SSH connections.

13. Domain Name System (DNS)

Definition: DNS is a hierarchical system that translates human-readable domain names (like www.example.com) into IP addresses.

Practical Example: If you want to verify the DNS resolution of a domain, you can use the command `nslookup www.example.com` in the command line to see the corresponding IP address.

14. DHCP (Dynamic Host Configuration Protocol)

Definition: DHCP is a network management protocol used to dynamically assign IP addresses to devices on a network.

Practical Example: You can configure your router to act as a DHCP server, automatically assigning IP addresses to devices on your network. It typically involves setting a range of addresses and defining lease duration.

15. Software Patch

Definition: A software patch is a piece of software designed to update or fix problems with a computer program or its supporting data.

Practical Example: On a Windows server, to apply patches, you might use the Windows Update feature, which can be initiated through the GUI or by using the command `wusa /install <patchname>.msu` in the command line.

16. System Logs

Definition: System logs are files that record events that occur within the operating system and applications, providing insight into system operation and troubleshooting.

Practical Example: In a Linux system, you can view system logs via the `journalctl` command. For example, `journalctl -b` displays logs from the current boot.

17. Load Balancing

Definition: Load balancing refers to the distribution of workloads across multiple resources to ensure no single resource is overwhelmed, optimizing resource use, maximizing throughput, and minimizing response time.

Practical Example: You might use a load balancer like HAProxy to distribute incoming HTTP requests across multiple web servers, improving performance and fault tolerance. You would configure it to direct traffic based on various algorithms, such as round-robin or least connections.

18. Monitoring

Definition: Monitoring involves regularly checking the state of IT resources to ensure they are functioning correctly and to detect issues before they impact users.

Practical Example: You could use tools like Nagios or Zabbix to monitor system performance and uptime. For instance, configuring Nagios involves editing the configuration files to specify which hosts and services to check.

19. Configuration Management

Definition: Configuration management refers to the practice of handling changes systematically so that a system maintains its integrity over time.

Practical Example: Tools like Ansible and Puppet can automate configuration management. For example, with Ansible, you might write a playbook to ensure all servers have a specific software package installed, and then execute it with the command `ansible-playbook install-package.yml`.

20. Security Policy

Definition: A security policy is a document that outlines the rules and measures an organization implements to protect its IT infrastructure and data.

Practical Example: You may draft a security policy that outlines password complexity requirements for users, which could stipulate a minimum length and the use of special characters. Regular audits would be scheduled to ensure compliance with this policy.

Understanding and effectively utilizing the terminology specific to system administration is fundamental for success in the field. This chapter has provided a comprehensive overview of the key terms and practical examples showcasing their application. As technology continues to evolve, staying informed about these terms will enhance your capabilities as a system administrator and improve your ability to manage complex IT environments effectively.

By mastering system administration terminology, you equip yourself with the necessary tools to tackle challenges and maintain efficient and secure systems.

Index

www.ingramcontent.com/pod-product-compliance
Lightning Source LLC
La Vergne TN
LVHW022346060326
832902LV00022B/4278